PUT OFF | PUT ON

Embracing God's Work of Sanctification in Your Life

TIM ARMSTRONG

DEDICATION

To
Him
Who denied Himself
and took up His cross
for us

To
Tom McCready
A reliable, unwavering friend

TABLE OF CONTENTS

1

Sanctification's Journey

*W*ork out your own salvation with fear and trembling.

What does it mean?

The phrase *work out your own salvation* has confused many for generations. It proves the importance of a fundamental aspect of Biblical interpretation — the importance of context.

Context is those events just before and after that will help us understand what a particular passage is saying. If we neglect context, we may miss the meaning. If we miss the meaning we're going to misinterpret. If we misinterpret we will misapply the message to our lives.

This passage — case and point — could lead to a grave mistake in regards to our salvation if we are not careful. We could mistakenly conclude that we participate in, or achieve, our own redemption. That couldn't be further from the truth.

Therefore, my beloved, as you have always obeyed, so now, not only as in my presence but much more in my absence, work out your own salvation with fear and trembling, for it is God who works in you, both to will and to work for his good pleasure (Philippians 2:12-13).

Starting with the phrase in question — *work out your salvation* — observe first what it does and doesn't say. The preposition in the phrase is key — it says work *out*, not at or for or to or towards. This is a vitally important distinction.

If we understood it as at, for, to or towards, we destroy the premise, *For by grace you have been saved through faith. And this is not your own doing; it is the gift of God, not a result of works, so that no one may boast. (Ephesians 2:8-9).*

Friend, your salvation is monergistic. What does that mean? The word comes from Greek origins. Do you see the *erg* in the middle it? In Greek *ergon* means work. So *mono-erg* is one working. God brought about your salvation. It was not through your works or efforts, but rather it is a gift from God. Monergistic. He's done the work.

So what then is Philippians 2:12-13 teaching? Not working at, for, to or toward, but rather working *out* your salvation.

I love what the great pastor and theologian, the late James Montgomery Boice said about this: "No one can work his salvation out unless God has already worked it in."

What we see here — and precisely what we'll see the scriptures bear out — this is not about our soul's salvation, but rather a call to work out our *sanctification.*

What is sanctification? The New Hampshire Baptist Confession of 1853 provides a succinct definition:

Sanctification is the process by which, according to the will of God, we are made partakers of his holiness; that it is a progressive work; that it is begun in regeneration; and that it is carried on in the hearts of believers by the presence and power of the Holy Spirit, the Sealer and Comforter, in the continual use of the appointed means-especially the Word of God, self-examination, self-denial, watchfulness, and prayer.

In Philippians 2:12-13 and in the old Baptist Confession above, sanctification is revealed to be a synergistic process. Monergistic — one working — salvation; synergistic — more than one working — sanctification.

Our sanctification is a process. As much as we're to be involved in it, God plays the crucial role. It is according to His will and found in His purpose, that we become more like Jesus Christ. The Holy Spirit carries it out in the hearts of believers, and we enter in by appropriating the means of God's Word, self-examination, self-denial, watchfulness and prayer.

It's really very simple. Sanctification is the process of becoming more like Jesus. In the passage before us, Paul is calling the Philippians to be like Christ. It's a familiar theme with him:

For just as you once presented your members as slaves to impurity and to lawlessness leading to more lawlessness, so now present your members as slaves to righteousness leading to sanctification (Romans 6:19).

For this is the will of God, your sanctification (1 Thessalonians 4:3).

So how do you do it? How do you work our your salvation?

The Greek word translated *work out* is katergazesthe. Try to say that fast and someone might offer you a tissue. You see the *erg* in the middle of it. This word means to work intensely, to carry on to completion, to accomplish. It depicts the kind of work a farmer does — up early, working long and hard hours, sweating, laboring to the point of exhaustion, and then up again before dawn the next day to do it all over.

Katergazesthe is a verb in present tense and imperative mood. In other words, it's a command with continual force behind it. It's a mandate: keep working out your maturation!

But here's the very good news about Philippians 2:12-13 — it doesn't just tell us what we should do, but it also shows us how we should do what we should do. Paul tells us to become more like Jesus. And he shows us how.

2

Sanctification's Process

Therefore, *my beloved, as you have always obeyed, so now, not only as in my presence but much more in my absence, work out your own salvation with fear and trembling, for it is God who works in you, both to will and to work for his good pleasure (Philippians 2:12-13).*

In this brief passage we discover two aspects of our sanctification: our role and God's role. Synergy. Man working alongside God.

The first factor is to *obey*. Practice obedience. Obedience to Christ is always the key factor. What did Jesus say? If you love me you will … keep my commands. He said it. It isn't something preachers made up.

The original word for obey is hypēkousate. Notice the *acou* in the middle? That is the root word for hearing in Greek, where we get the English word acoustic. And the prefix *hypo* at the beginning — it means under; think of a hypodermic needle that goes under the skin. So you have a word that carries the connotation of *hearing under*, or placing yourself under the direction of what you've heard. Or … obey.

In Romans 12, Paul spoke of sanctification as a process of being transformed, of being renewed. It requires our obedience, placing ourselves in submission. It requires discipline. It looks like the dedication and hard work of an athlete.

It's no wonder so many of the apostle's metaphors are sports-related. Here's one example:

Every athlete exercises self-control in all things. They do it to receive a perishable wreath, but we an imperishable. So I do not run aimlessly; I do not box as one beating the air. But I discipline my body and keep it under control, lest after preaching to others I myself should be disqualified (1 Corinthians 9:25-27).

Paul puts the process of becoming like Christ in athletic jargon. He gives an example from the world of track and field, in Olympic games terms.

Now I'm not an athlete. That is obvious to those who've met me. Whether you are or not, I dare say it's clear to us all: If you want to win an Olympic race you have to exercise self-control, self-discipline. You have to train hard for years. That's the picture Paul is painting.

He took it a step further, using the metaphor of a boxer. Do you see the phrase *I strike a blow to my body*? Talk about the importance of context! Did you know there was a whole era where priests and monks took this phrase literally and beat their own bodies bloody? Paul isn't calling you to physically harm yourself. In the context of an athletic metaphor, he's saying, "think of your life like a race and train accordingly."

Paul clarified: followers of Jesus Christ are pursuing an imperishable wreath! This isn't some wreath of olive leaves, or plastic participation trophy you'll throw in a closet that will disintegrate over time. This prize reaches into eternity.

Looking back to the text In Philippians 2, please don't miss that Paul started by addressing the people as *my beloved*. God has given you a name — beloved one, or loved by God. And isn't that a marvelous segue heading into a passage about working out your salvation?

The command to be obedient is introduced with a reminder: you are loved by God. We will not always obey. Sometimes we will stumble and fall. It doesn't negate the truth: you are the beloved of God. It actually serves as motivation: you are loved; therefore, you want to obey. When you fail, you are loved; you want to return to your journey.

And that leads to a second key factor: *personalizing our submission.* Look at how Paul rolled out this instruction: As you have always obeyed (past), so now (present), but much more when I'm not here (future), make it your own. And the fact that Paul speaks past, present and into the future, it's clear that there come points in time when you must lead yourself, or be self-led in the direction of obeying.

I believe discipleship relationships are a great thing. Having said that, I've seen — and I'm sure you've seen — people who have been in those relationships for years and are no more spiritually mature than when they started. You cannot be indebted to someone else without, at some point, making it personal, taking on your own path of maturity.

Allow the apostle Peter to remind you: you were called, *"according to the foreknowledge of God the Father, in the sanctification of the Spirit, for obedience to Jesus Christ"* (1 Peter 1:2a).

Are you making it personal? Are you doing this? What's your plan? Do you have a plan?

Realize, too, that plans ebb and flow. Some seasons run deeper than others. Some are less fervent. I've always enjoyed a connection with nature. There is almost no place I feel closer to God than when I can be out hunting. I'll climb up in a tree stand, turn off the cell phone, break out a little pocket size Bible and really commune with God in His creation. It's a really sweet time. But it's only for a season. I can't stay in the tree stand forever. Life rushes back in.

So it is with this sanctification journey. There will be times when you sense God's work in your life and move with Him. There will be other times when you feel a little distant — and long to get back to the sweet spot. Worry not. It's a process. Own it. You must personalize your submission.

Begin by *cultivating an awe of God.* And this is a third key factor in your part of sanctification — a deep and abiding reverence for your God.

At the end of verse 12, Paul says, work out your salvation *with fear and trembling.* In the Greek, fear is phobou, where we get the word phobia. When you match it with the Greek word tromou, translated trembling in English, you have a picture of profound respect for, and a healthy fear of offending your Lord.

Let God tell you Himself: *"This is the one to whom I will look: he who is humble and contrite in spirit and trembles at my word"* (Isaiah 66:2b).

Has this happened to you? You're reading along in Scripture and you come across a verse, and something like a cold chill rolls down your spine? Or perhaps you're in church and you hear a sermon or a lesson, someone shares a word and you feel like it was intended just for you? When you recognize it, trembling is putting yourself under the word, submitting to it.

The author of Hebrews said, *"it is a fearful thing to fall into the hands of a living God"* (Hebrews 10:31). Yes, He is love, grace and He is our Father. He is also God of the universe. And what do we see in the Bible? A righteous reverence. People don't waltz into His presence in cavalier spirit. No. You see them fall flat on their faces before a holy God, in fact a holy, holy, holy God — a thrice-holy God. Beloved, tremble.

Now you may be thinking, how can I do this sanctification thing? I'm not strong enough. You're right. You're not. But you're not alone on this journey. You've got your part to play, but more importantly,

God is at work in your sanctification.

Whereas verse 12 calls us to *obey*, to *personalize our submission* and to *cultivate a healthy reverence* for God, verse 13 alerts us to His role — particular aspects of God's sanctifying work in us.

… for it is God who works in you, both to will and to work for his good pleasure (Philippians 2:13).

It is God who works in you. I cannot overstate the importance of those words. They reassure, they underscore, you are not alone in this journey. You're not left to yourself, your abilities and your own devices to pull this off. God is empowering you.

Again we see the word *work*. It is different here than the word in verse 12. Here the Greek word is energōn, a present tense participle in the active voice. It speaks of an operative work; God is actively and continually at work energizing you in this direction. It's a cause and effect sort of relationship — because He's at work, progress occurs. This is the kind of work that brings something from one point to another. Do you see that? He is at work in you, bringing *you* from one point to another. This is who He is; it's His heart, His will, His purpose. You know what He says in His Word:

For the eyes of the Lord run to and fro throughout the whole earth, to give strong support to those whose heart is blameless toward him (2 Chronicles 16:9).

Even to your old age I am he, and to gray hairs I will carry you. I have made, and I will bear; I will carry and will save (Isaiah 46:4).

Aren't those *I will* statements beautiful? I will carry. I will bear. I will save. Count on it. He energizes you in working out your salvation, your sanctification.

The rest of verse 13 gives us a glimpse into how God works in or energizes our sanctification. He works in you *to will* — in other words He works on your mind and heart, giving you new desires toward holiness. That's not something we muster up on our own like a New Year's resolution. You can no more will yourself to become holy than you can will yourself to become a banana.

The psalmist gave us a real insight into the process: *Delight yourself in the Lord, and he will give you the desires of your heart (Psalm 37:4).*

It goes without saying, this isn't a promise that God will serve you up whatever you want — that would be wrangling this badly out of context. Rather, God is at work in us, changing the desires of our hearts, birthing within us desire for holiness we've never known before and couldn't know without Him.

The continuation of the thought at the end of verse 12: to will and *to work.* The energizing work God is doing moves from volition to deeds. He not only rewrites our desires, but empowers those desires to bear deeds. This is sanctification: moving you into a walk of righteousness. It is like pastor and Bible scholar John McArthur has said, "God gives us a holy discontent while at the same time holy aspirations, that we might think and act like Christ."

Why? You see it right there at the end of the passage: *for His good pleasure.* It brings your Heavenly Father great pleasure, great satisfaction, when you work out your salvation. It's how He's intended it to be; how He intended you to be. Your role. His role. Synergized. That's your sanctification. Let's take a deeper look.

3

Sanctification's Identity

Having considered our sanctification from two sides — our role and God's role, our work and His — let me call attention to another important passage on this matter, Ephesians 4, where the apostle Paul begins:

I therefore, a prisoner for the Lord, urge you to walk in a manner worthy of the calling to which you have been called (Ephesians 4:1).

I recently shared this verse with my children. We often read a passage of scripture before bed, and this one seemed so very appropriate. I want them to be mindful of the call to continue to walk after the Lord. As they enter into the world — school, friends, their peer group, the many different options that will be presented to them — I want this to be fresh in their minds. This is what we do as parents. It's living out the direction God gave in Deuteronomy 6.

It's in that spirit, I believe, that Paul spoke this admonition to the church at Ephesus. He begins by issuing a call to the Ephesian believers. The word *urge* is actually a little bit of word play. It is parakalō in Greek, the prefix para (alongside) and the root kaleo (call). So the apostle is calling those reading this letter along, to walk in a manner worthy of the greater call upon their lives. He goes on to describe what this looks like:

... with all humility and gentleness, with patience, bearing with one another in love, eager to maintain the unity of the Spirit in the bond of peace (Ephesians 4:2-3).

That sounds great, but how do you do it? Good news. Here again, like in Philippians 2, Paul tells us what we should do and then goes on to show us how we should do what we should do.

Now this I say and testify in the Lord, that you must no longer walk as the Gentiles do, in the futility of their minds (Ephesians 4:17).

First, he says, you must no longer walk as the Gentiles do. It begs a question, doesn't it? How do the Gentiles walk?

The word Gentile is used three different ways in the New Testament. Sometimes it appears referring to an individual who is outside of Judaism. Sometimes it is used to represent a nation outside Judaism. But it is also used to represent a category of people, and that is how it is used here — don't walk like those who are Gentiles. Remember that context is our friend, and context goes on to explain the Gentiles do not know God. So in essence Paul is saying, don't walk as if you don't know God.

Paul's analogy would have been very clear to the Ephesian believers. Ephesus was, in its day, a society of stark contrasts. It was certainly a beautiful city, one of the greatest in all the Roman Empire. It was also the most pagan of societies.

Not long ago, I took a group of people to Ephesus, which is ancient Asia Minor, and now modern day Turkey. Thousands of years after its collapse, it is still a glorious city. As you walk through, you can imagine its gleaming pathways, its mansions off on the hillside, its tremendous library. We walked in the Agora, which was similar to a shopping mall and the amphitheater which seats more than 10,000. But what is most striking, even to this day, is what remains of the temple of Artemis.

It is in ruins today. But it is massive in scope. And it is mind-boggling, really. This huge complex was dedicated to one god,

Artemis, also known as Diana, the fertility goddess.

Here at the center of Ephesus is this temple that actually represents the lifestyle of the people of Ephesus in ancient times. In its day the temple employed hundreds of male and female prostitutes. People from all over Roman society would come to Ephesus, and go to the temple to worship. The way they would express their worship was by engaging in the most illicit behavior imaginable with the temple prostitutes. Fifth century Greek philosopher, Heraclitus — a pagan himself — referred to Ephesus as "The darkness of vileness," saying, "The morals were lower than animals and the inhabitants of Ephesus were fit only to be drowned." Can you imagine that?

This is the culture Paul was speaking into. And he says to the Ephesian believers, I don't want you to walk like the Gentiles around you. I don't want you to live your life like this. They understood. They had come out of this lifestyle. They knew paganism; they knew idol worship. Paul knew of the temptation they faced because of the culture they were in. They could easily slip back into that lifestyle. Understand his admonition against that backdrop.

What does he say? Don't walk as the Gentiles. Paul gave four characteristics of that particular society. See if you can spot them in the text:

Now this I say and testify in the Lord, that you must no longer walk as the Gentiles do, in the futility of their minds. They are darkened in their understanding, alienated from the life of God because of the ignorance that is in them, due to their hardness of heart. They have become callous and have given themselves up to sensuality, greedy to practice every kind of impurity (Ephesians 4:17-19).

Can you pick out the four? They walked *in the futility of their minds.* They walked *with darkened understanding.* They walked *in calloused sensuality.* And they walked *greedy to practice every kind of impurity.*

It's worthwhile to pause there for a moment and make a quick observation. Those four phrases — futility of mind, darkened understanding, calloused sensuality and greedy to impurity — these characteristics encompass *thinking, reasoning, feeling* and *action*. In other words, Paul is touching life at every level.

It is worthwhile to go through them one at a time. What we're doing, in essence, is deconstructing a life that used to be, so we can construct a life of what we are, now, called to be. Do you follow me? Paul is calling us to walk after Jesus Christ. But there must be a sense of deconstruction of the life that we once lived in order to construct a life we should be walking in.

Let's start with thinking. No longer walk as the Gentiles do *in the futility of their minds*. Now this word futility in the original language means emptiness, void, void of substance.

We embrace the inspired, infallible and inerrant Word of God. But it wasn't written in English. So where we can go back and the original language helps us to understand the meaning and the mindset behind words, it gives us a fuller picture.

This is a great example — the word futility. The way we use the word in English, many images could come to mind. To understand that the original conveys the idea of emptiness or void of substance clarifies the picture. Hear what he is saying: believers and unbelievers think differently. Where spiritual things are concerned, the Gentile mind has nothing. Nada. Empty. But believer, you have been given the mind of Christ. This is why scripture places such a high priority on the idea of renewing your mind.

In 1 Corinthians 2, Paul says there is a wisdom that is of the Spirit, it comes from Jesus Christ; and there is the wisdom of this world. The two are not the same. Look how he explains it:

The natural person does not accept the things of the Spirit of God, for they are folly to him, and he is not able to understand them because they are spiritually discerned. The spiritual person judges all things, but is himself to be judged by no one. "For who has understood the mind of the Lord so as to instruct him?" But we have the mind of Christ (1 Corinthians 2:14-16).

Do you see there is a difference? In his letter to Titus, Paul said it this way:

To the pure, all things are pure, but to the defiled and unbelieving, nothing is pure; but both their minds and their consciences are defiled (Titus 1:15).

The world, the flesh, humanity — that which we once were a part of — their minds and consciences are defiled. But we have the mind of Christ! The old you, the old mind, has gone. It's been done away with. You don't think the same. Paul is saying, don't think like the Gentiles who don't know God. Because you do know Him!

From thinking, he moves right into reasoning. What did he say? The Gentiles are *darkened in their understanding, alienated from the life of God because of the ignorance that is in them.* There is so much here. It's a stinging indictment. Let's take an overview first, and then we'll dig a little deeper.

What happens when you don't know the difference between what is right and what is wrong? What happens when you interchange what is right for what is wrong, and what is wrong for what is right? Woe to you! By the way, that is exactly what Isaiah the prophet said: *Woe to those who call evil good and good evil, who put darkness for light and light for darkness, who put bitter for sweet and sweet for bitter! (Isaiah 5:20)* Woe to those who don't understand.

The essence of the Christian life, the essence of the Christian worldview, is that you and I believe in absolute truth. If there is no absolute truth, what governs our morality? We govern our morality. Once we throw out absolute truth then we become the standard for truth — and what truth is for me might be vastly different from what truth is for you. So we can argue about whose truth is better because we have no absolute. And then what we have is a culture thrown into chaos without absolute truth. Sounds a lot like the times we're living in, doesn't it?

A society that says any lifestyle, no matter how abhorrent it might be to one, is perfectly fine for another — lives by the credo "mind your own business," and "mind your own truth."

Let's be clear, though. Our culture is not nearly as bad as the culture that Paul was writing to. We might be tempted to think things cannot get any worse. Yes, they can. And they will. It shouldn't surprise us. It should drive us to our knees, not in judgment, but praying that God would draw the hearts and minds of those who are Gentile-like, who do not yet know Him, to Jesus Christ so they might understand truth and be set free.

You have been set free. Do you understand that? Not free to judge. But free to love, and to call on God the Father to rain down his mercy, as he did on us, to those who don't know him yet. We stand for truth, but we do it in love. He is the judge. We are people who have been given mercy and the mercy is wrapped into divine truth. The Light has come; we now know how to walk. Paul's message to the Ephesians and ultimately to us: don't walk like that any more. That's not who you are.

To dig a little deeper, consider the flow of this text to its outcome. He says they were darkened — and in Greek that is a perfect passive participle. Try to say that three times fast. What does it mean? It means that something that occurred in the past still has ramifications into the present, and will in the future.

Think on that for a moment. Darken. The word in Greek speaks of the continuing condition of spiritual darkness. They are in spiritual darkness, and unless and until God enlightens their minds, draws them to Himself, they will remain in continual spiritual darkness. By the way, you and I cannot do one thing about that. We can argue and we can defend until we are blue in the face, but unless and until God does a work in their hearts, their ears are closed. Their mind is ... darkened. That is their reality. What is the consequence? The inability to understand.

That's the next word in the flow. *Understanding*, here, is the idea of deep thought. They cannot think deeply. But it's important to mention — and context clarifies — we're not saying they are whole-heartedly ignorant, that they cannot think deeply on any subject or matter. Of course they can. The common grace of God allows all of mankind, even those who do not know God, to reason and think deeply. But they have a stopping point when it comes to the divine. They cannot think deeply with a sense of understanding about God.

To be clear, unbelievers can think about God. A good many might even suppose they've thought deeply about God. They have, however, a deep misunderstanding about their understanding. Because of their spiritual ignorance, they don't know what they don't know. Better yet, they don't know Who they don't know.

The word *ignorance*, here, refers to moral blindness. They are blind, and they are the blind leading the blind. You can see this comes full circle. The flow continues into the last phrase, which sums it all up: *due to their hardness of heart*. This word *hardness* carries the idea of being in rock-solid calcification.

Their hearts have become calcified. Their reasoning is outside of God. They have a limit to their thinking, and in their understanding of God. They need divine heart surgery, a new heart only God can give.

How you think and how you reason ultimately impacts your feelings and your actions. That is still the case for us, by the way. We might be redeemed, but if we are not guarding our minds, if we are not guarding our hearts — which Proverbs says is the wellspring of life — we begin to shift our thinking away from Christ and towards Gentile-like thinking. This is why Paul calls believers in Ephesus to be very careful how they think and reason.

Paul calls them — and us — to vigilance. It's the same call expanded in Ephesians that he gives the Philippians: *Work out your salvation in fear and trembling.* How do you do that? Through your mind, through your thinking and through your reasoning.

Take hold of this. Remember what he says in Philippians: *Have this mind among yourselves, which is yours in Christ Jesus (Philippians 2:5).*

Beloved, we must guard our minds and the portals to our minds, our eyes and ears. We live in a Gentile-like society, propagating its own version of truth and spirituality. We must be wise. I'm not advocating we retreat into hiding from big-bad culture cooties. I'm saying be wise — just because something is legal doesn't mean it is in our best interest. Paul said that himself: *All things are lawful for me, but not all things are helpful (1 Corinthians 6:12).* Wisdom.

I see people — you've seen them too — who run headlong into our culture, embracing what they see, read and hear, bringing it into their lifestyle. That's not who you are in Christ. Your relationship with Christ is your new lifestyle. When you see something that starts to move your thinking away from Christ, you guard your heart. Don't go down that way.

Isn't that what we do with our children? We're constantly monitoring their intake. What is going into their little minds? What's going in through their eyes? Even our society has some semblance of this — movie ratings, for instance. There is G. Do they even make G-rated movies anymore? There's PG and PG13. I've always found that distinction fascinating. It's as if society is telling me my parental guidance is only necessary to a point — at 13 there's a threshold. Then, of course, there is R-rated. Now I am not here to be a movie critic. My point is to say, just as we are careful with our children, what they put in their minds, we have to be careful what we put into our minds. Just because it's on the top 10 best-seller list doesn't mean you ought to read it. Just because it is on the radio station doesn't mean you need it on your playlist.

I'm really not being a prude. Hear my heart. Hear the apostle Paul's heart in these passages. Hear our Heavenly Father's heart. That's what we're all after.

Michelle and I recently had these discussions about what we see channeling into our home through our television set. And we wonder, how much are we allowing a Gentile-like culture to come streaming into our home and create its own guidelines, its own morals, and its own realities. You know what I mean. It creeps up on you. You didn't just throw open the windows. It filters in through cracks and crevices and slowly engulfs.

In verse 19, the flow moves from thinking and reasoning to feelings. The word *callus* means to grow or become insensible. It literally means to get beyond feeling. Their thinking and reasoning was so skewed, their feelings had passed the point of feeling.

John Calvin in his commentary described it this way: *"Unmoved by the approaching judgment of God, whom they offend, they go on at their ease, and fearlessly indulge without restraint in the pleasures of sin. No shame is felt, no regard to character is maintained. The gnawing of a guilty conscience, tormented by the dread of the Divine judgment, may be compared to the porch of hell; but such hardened security as this — is a whirlpool which swallows up and destroys."*

This is why Paul tells us *work out our salvation with fear and trembling.* When I read this, I think, *O God, please don't let this be me!* I don't want to get to a point where I am past feeling. Where I can't hear the spirit of what Paul says; where my conscience is seared. I don't want to be past the point so guilt no longer comes raging into my life, where I have pushed it so far away that it's no longer felt. This is what Paul warns the Ephesians; this is exactly what your culture is like — they're past thinking, reasoning and feeling.

Ultimately the flow leads to this fourth characteristic: *openness to any action*, an appetite for anything, really. At the end of verse 19, Paul zeroes in. I suspect this was in response to the temple of Artemis, which had spread throughout that society, become its culture. He speaks specifically of sensuality. He says *greedy*, but it's not greedy as in a financial greed, rather it's a greed to practice every kind of impurity. In other words, they have an insatiable appetite and lustful desire for sensuality. The idea is one of unbridled self-indulgence in sex. That is what he is addressing here. This part really does resemble our cultural setting today, doesn't it? We are bombarded by sensuality. We are driven to every kind of impurity.

Paul says to the Ephesians, like he would say to us: Don't get swept up in the current of the culture. Why?

But that is not the way you learned Christ! (Ephesians 4:20)

That's not who you are. That's the old you. That's not the new you. *But*. Here is a transition. Having deconstructed, Paul is now ready to start the construction project on the sanctification of the believer.

Do you remember what he said to the Corinthians? *Therefore, if anyone is in Christ, he is a new creation. The old has passed away; behold, the new has come (2 Corinthians 5:17)*. Do you believe it?

Beloved, don't act like the old you. Don't dabble in the Gentile-like lifestyle. In your thinking, your reasoning, in your feeling, in your actions, that's not who you are in Christ.

It's time to follow Paul as he launches into the characteristics that should define our sanctification. This is often where people say they understand it philosophically. They understand the target, what we are trying to get to. But what we need is the nuts and bolts. What am I to do in the process of sanctification? Thankfully, it's all here.

4

Sanctification's Blessing

There is a new you.

The text is calling you forward into the construction project of a righteous life.

Now I love that metaphor because it helps us. Perhaps you've seen these remodeling shows on television. The first thing they do is drop a big dumpster in the driveway, rip down and rip out all the old décor and fill that dumpster to overflowing.

We have to deconstruct what is in order to construct what needs to be. We have to deconstruct that Gentile-like lifestyle so that we can construct a lifestyle based on righteousness. So think of it this way: we are in a remodeling project.

Are you ready to build?

But that is not the way you learned Christ! — assuming that you have heard about him and were taught in him, as the truth is in Jesus, to put off your old self, which belongs to your former manner of life and is corrupt through deceitful desires, and to be renewed in the spirit of your minds, and to put on the new self, created after the likeness of God in true righteousness and holiness (Ephesians 4:20-24).

This passage begins with an assumption. Do you see it? The assumption includes three verbs, he says, you *learned* Christ, you *heard* about Him, and you were *taught* in Him. Paul begins with the assumption that the people he's writing to have true faith.

We should examine ourselves as to whether or not we are in the true faith. Paul didn't mince words. He said: *Examine yourselves, to see whether you are in the faith. Test yourselves. Or do you not realize this about yourselves, that Jesus Christ is in you? — unless indeed you fail to meet the test! (2 Corinthians 13:5)*

We ought to look in the mirror, asking: Am I truly in the faith? Learned. Heard. Taught. Those three verbs form an excellent litmus test.

First, he said you *learned* Christ. It means you've learned to a point of personal understanding. This is not the type of learning that my high school daughters often go through. When they have to read a book, they'll buy the Cliff Notes. Do you know what Cliff Notes are? They summarize what's in the book, to prepare you for the test. Once the test is passed in, you forget all about the book. You don't care to retain that knowledge any longer.

That's not the type of learning in view here. This learning brings you to personal understanding. It's more than facts. It's more than doctrine. It has a personal relationship at the heart of it. You learned Christ in a personal way. More than just something you know, it's Someone you are getting to know. It's an abiding kind of learning.

Next, he said you *heard* about Him. The word heard, ēkousate, means not only to hear, but also to submit. In other words, you've learned about Him, and now you're willing to surrender yourself to Him. You see it's one thing to know facts and quite another to internalize them and determine they are going to govern your life.

Finally, he said you were *taught* in Him. In Greek, edidachthēte paints a picture of a continual process of learning. What a great picture of authentic faith. You've heard about Christ. You've made it personal. Now you're continuing in Christ.

On the matter of continuing in Christ, do you understand that you're a part of a process that was started by the apostles, was handed down to you, and now you must hand down to others? That's the direction Paul gave to Timothy: *You then, my child, be strengthened by the grace that is in Christ Jesus, and what you have heard from me in the presence of many witnesses entrust to faithful men who will be able to teach others also (2 Timothy 2:1-2).*

Do you realize that's the process of the spiritual life? This is what the reality that Jesus Christ is alive within you looks like. It's something you've heard, you've learned, you've internalized, and now you're part of the process of learning and passing it forward. It doesn't matter how old you are; you never stop. It doesn't matter how young you are; you never stop learning and passing forward. Are you in that process? If it stops with you, you failed. The call is to continue passing the baton.

You say I don't know much, that's fine. Find someone who knows less than you and teach them all you know. Find someone who knows more than you do, learn everything they have to offer. That's part of the process of learning. Here's the picture of the saving faith. Remember the context: Paul is contrasting the Gentile-life to the Christ-follower's life.

One more thought on the phrase *assuming that you have heard about him* before we move on. In case you have doubts about where you stand …

Sometimes people have said to me, "I'm not sure if I'm a believer." I'll ask about their life. Do you know about Jesus Christ? Do you understand His death, burial and resurrection? Do you understand that it's not something you must do, but rather faith comes by hearing, by believing that it's a gift from God? "Yes," they'll say, "I understand all that." Finally I'll ask, Do you have a desire to walk in righteousness? "Yes." I tell them to relax. You have all the characteristics of one who has authentic faith.

We may not always be able to carry out our righteousness as

clearly and consistently as we'd like, but if our internal desire is to be obedient to the God, we've come to know Jesus Christ, and to walk after Him, relax. Enjoy the salvation that has been given to you … and continue on.

The reformers identified three components to saving faith. Now to put this in context, when I speak of the reformers, I'm speaking of the Protestant Reformation of the 16th century. We are Protestants, or if you like, we are protesters. What are we protesting? It goes all the way back to the 16th century when reformers began protesting the Roman Catholic Church. Catholic doctrine had moved away from the gospel. The reformers protested, hoping to reform the church, bring it back to the original gospel message of the scriptures. True saving faith isn't built upon counsels or popes or the church. It rests upon Jesus Christ.

So those three terms — the first is *notitia*. It's a Latin word that means the knowledge of faith. It's very similar to what see in Ephesians 4, we *learned* Christ. Notitia faith always has an object that we must embrace — that is Jesus Christ. To believe in Jesus we must first know of Him.

In his letter to the church in Rome, Paul asked, *"How then will they call on him in whom they have not believed? And how are they to believe in him of whom they have never heard? And how are they to hear without someone preaching? (Romans 10:14)*

It's this whole paradigm: we must proclaim what is needed to be known, because that knowing is vitally important; that is notitia.

Knowledge alone, however, is not enough. It's just the starting point. You must also affirm that truth, just as we have been learning. Saving faith, the reformers said, requires an *assensus*. Another Latin word, assensus refers to a conviction that the content you've come to know is absolutely true. It's something we hear and which rings true within us. In practical terms, our spirit is met by the Holy Spirit, so there is a confirmation that takes place.

To be sure, there are many who have knowledge of the factual contents of scripture but do not have the conviction that the content is true. They have knowledge, but haven't moved it from their mind to their souls; they haven't had a connection between the Spirit of God and their own human spirit to assure them of its truthfulness.

James 2:19 says, *You believe that God is one; you do well. Even the demons believe — and shudder!*

The demons have knowledge, they even believe that it's true. But they shudder. It's interesting, that word shudder means that the hair on the back of their necks stand up when they think about Jesus Christ, and the truth of who He is. I bet you didn't know demons had hair on their back of their necks. That's a freebie for you.

So there's *notitia*, there's *assensus*, then finally, a third Latin word, there's *fiducia*. Fiducia is where your personal reliance upon and trust in Jesus Christ is discernable to the watching world. And this is really the point Paul is making: You are a Christ follower; there ought to be a demonstration that your faith is true and authentic. You ought to walk like one.

Having deconstructed the Gentile-like life, he moves on to the matter of construction. What are the characteristics of a Christ-follower's lifestyle? Paul is going to give us the three characteristics of sanctification. In other words, the remodeling dumpster is full out in the driveway. Now is the time when you spread the plans before you — time to bring in the new.

Nuts and bolts, remember? What we must do? Because, that's what's needed; that's what we desire. We want to know, "What is it that I must do to grow spiritually?"

Construction begins in verse 22, *put off your old self, which belongs to your former manner of life and is corrupt through deceitful desires.*

Step one: Put off the actions of the old self. What does it mean? It means, don't live your former life. Set it aside. It makes no sense to continue in that former way of life. It's over. That's not you anymore. You're a person of true faith. Don't act like a person who has no faith. Put it off.

It gives us imagery that is helpful, something to which we can all relate. We all know what it is to take off old items of clothing and discard them. Do you ever go through your closet and do that? Something doesn't fit anymore so you put it aside or put it in a bag, perhaps pass it on to someone else.

I can remember when most of my clothing was the same size, from about my junior year in high school until my early to mid-thirties. I was a size 31-32. But somehow ... I guess I can blame it on seminary ... or marriage ... all of a sudden, nothing fit anymore! I went from a 31-32 to a 36, and I was growing.

Mid-thirties, mid-forties ... I'm cleaning out my closet again. In your mid-fifties, you even look at food, and you gain weight! So, you're taking your old clothes off ... those are your old clothes; they don't fit you anymore.

That's the imagery that Paul uses. Your old life and your old lifestyle; the way you used to act; the way you used to think; the way you used to talk; the things you used to desire — those things aren't you anymore. They don't fit! Put them off. It's even weightier than that. In Greek the word rendered put off, apothesthai, means to renounce. So put them off, and then don't go back to them.

You know how that goes. You find the blouse or the trousers that don't fit anymore, but you really, really like them. You sort of bury them deeper in the closet, thinking maybe one day they'll fit again, or one day they'll come back in style. Don't do it! Mind you, I'm extrapolating the metaphor here, talking about sanctification. If you want to hold on to a pair of parachute pants or a Member's Only jacket from the 1980s … I can't help you.

But Paul does say to look forward! Speaking of the sanctification construction project in another place, he begins: *If then you have been raised with Christ, seek the things that are above, where Christ is, seated at the right hand of God. Set your minds on things that are above, not on things that are on earth (Colossians 3:1-2).*

Sound familiar? There's the assumption — if you are a Christ follower. It's what we just looked at: set your mind on things above.

Here again is the language — put off and put on: *Put to death therefore what is earthly in you: sexual immorality, impurity, passion, evil desire, and covetousness, which is idolatry. On account of these the wrath of God is coming. In these you too once walked, when you were living in them (Colossians 3:5-7).*

You once walked. Past tense. This is a description of the old you; the way you used to clothe your life. He continues: *But now you must put them all away: anger, wrath, malice, slander, and obscene talk from your mouth. Do not lie to one another, seeing that you have put off the old self with its practices (Colossians 3:8-9).*

Now watch as the direction shifts. It's the same concept, same imagery, but the direction changes: *Put on the new self, which is being renewed in knowledge after the image of its creator (Colossians 3:10).*

Look again at the way Paul describes the exchange in Ephesians: *Put off your old self, which belongs to your former manner of life and is corrupt through deceitful desires (Ephesians 4:22).*

He clarifies again that this old self belongs to your former manner of life, which is — don't miss this — *corrupt through deceitful desires.* In that old way of thinking, the old way of ordering your life, old desires were deceiving you. So the admonition here is don't go back to the days of deception.

Now, parenthetically — and we must do this with a very loving, non-judgmental spirit — when we meet people who do not know the Lord, or, as I like to phrase it, do not *yet* know the Lord, we see them make choices we might have made in the past. Their choices are deceiving them. You can peer in and see it — those choices won't bring them freedom, won't bring them hope, won't bring them fulfillment. How do you know it? Because you've been there.

But the light has shone in your life. And that should move your heart to compassion. Love should compel you; that they might come to know Jesus.

Don't go back to those things that deceive. Have you noticed how when you fall, when you sin, you immediately know it? You see it as deception. There is sometimes even a physical sense of being unclean. That's a sensation that only those who are following Christ understand.

We have a glorious reality: *If we confess our sins, he is faithful and just to forgive us our sins and to cleanse us from all unrighteousness (1 John 1:9).* The old self must be put off and put away. Embrace a fresh start.

To put off your old self … and to be renewed in the spirit of your minds, and to put on the new self, created after the likeness of God in true righteousness and holiness (Ephesians 4:22a, 23-24).

Notice the transition. Put off the actions of the old self. And, then, renew *the spirit of my mind.* What does that mean? It is one of the most awkward phrases in the New Testament. It only appears here.

So it begs the question: What was he getting at?

Let's parse it out. He says, *and to be renewed.* The word rendered *be renewed* is ananeousthaia, a verb. It's a specific verb; it's a present, passive, infinitive verb. It speaks of continual action. Your mind is to continually be renewed. How is your mind renewed? It is renewed from the old self to the new self. This is like a bridge.

The way you know what to put off and what to put on comes through the renewing of your mind. How is your mind renewed? Through God's Word. That's what you do — you don't base it on your own thinking or your own theories. You don't base it on somebody else's concepts or ideas. You go right to the Word of God. What does The Word of God tell me? That's the foundation upon which you build your life.

You have to renew your mind around God's Book. You study this Book; you memorize this Book; you learn this Book. Why? Because it's part of renewing your mind.

How often have you studied something and memorized something from this Book and, in a very short period of time, you've forgotten it? It happens to me all the time. I'm dumbfounded by this! Especially when I think of some of the things I remember without even trying.

I recall a vacation when I was a little boy. We stopped at a rest area and I went into the restroom where there was some *poetry* written on the bathroom wall. Now if you've never experienced this, let me give you some advice: the great poets of our day are not writing on bathroom walls.

But, I was a kid. I read the rhymes on the wall. I could share it with you to this day, rhyme and meter, and never miss a word. Ask me a Bible passage I memorized just five days ago, and I will stumble and stammer all over the place. Why is that? My mind likes to move to its fallen nature. What do I have to do? I must renew it. I must constantly be renewing my mind. You know what I'm talking about.

Can you imagine the impact on your life if God spoke directly to you? You would never forget that moment. I was thinking about that recently as I was reading through the book of Judges. I came to that classic passage in chapter 7 where Gideon is going out to fight the Midianites. Do you remember the story?

The Midianites were assembled in the north and there were 120,000 of them. Gideon has the Israelite army, and they numbered

32,000. They're outnumbered 4 to 1. God spoke to Gideon, saying, "Gideon, you're going to go to battle with the Midianites. But, I don't want you to win and think that you were the one that caused the victory. So, I want you to go to the men and I want you to say very simply, 'If you're fearful because we're outnumbered 4 to 1 then you can go home.'"

Can you imagine having that kind of opportunity? I'm not proud of this but I would have probably gone home. Outnumbered 4 to 1?

Twenty-two thousand took him up on the offer and left. Just like that, Gideon's army was down to 10,000. Do the math — now they're outmatched 12 to 1. What do you think Gideon was thinking? I'll tell you. He was hanging on to, "God said …" because he readied for battle. But God came to him again and said, "You still have too many."

God directed, "This is what I want you to do. I want you to take your army down to the spring of Herod," which is a beautiful location, by the way. I stop there whenever we're traveling through Israel, when we're on guided tour, and I can take you to the hill where the Midianites were, to the valley where the Israelites were and to this very spring.

"Take them to the spring," God said, "and watch them; we're going to divide them. Those who get down on one knee, and with their hand, dip into the water, separate them from those who get down on all four, and actually put their lips into the stream." Gideon did as he was told. 9,700 men got down on all four to drink. Only 300 got down on one knee to lap it up. God said, "There's your army. Take the 300. That's all you're going to need."

God wanted it to be absolutely clear that He was the One giving the enemy into Gideon's hands. Now, you would not believe that or act upon that unless you were absolutely convinced that you'd heard God's Voice.

How do you defeat an army of 120,000 trained soldiers with 300 men? I'll tell you how: you obey God's voice.

You say, "If only I had God speaking to me." You do! It's right here in the Bible. If God says it, your response needs to be, "I'm going to obey it." Why? Because you can trust Him. It's been proven over and over again.

If you follow your deceitful desires, it will lead you to destruction. If you follow the truth of God, it will lead you towards righteousness. You want to grow in your Christian life? You *put off* and you *renew your mind* through God's Word.

And, when you renew your mind, then you're ready for the next step: *To put on the new self, created after the likeness of God in true righteousness and holiness (Ephesians 4:24).*

Put on in Greek, endysasthai, is an action of putting on a piece of clothing. We have come full circle, haven't we? It's the same thing Paul said to the Philippians: *Work out your salvation.* It's action based.

How do we know what is righteous? How do we know what is holy? We read on. Paul's message here in Ephesians 4 unfolds very much like it did in Colossians 3: *Therefore, having put away falsehood, let each one of you speak the truth with his neighbor, for we are members one of another (Ephesians 4:25).*

Put away falsehood and tell the truth. You don't lie because we're truth-tellers now. Do you see the exchange?

Here's an even clearer example: *Let the thief no longer steal, but rather let him labor, doing honest work with his own hands, so that he may have something to share with anyone in need (Ephesians 4:28).*

Talk about a transformed life! You were once a thief. Stop stealing. Put your hands to honest work so you can bless others. Again, don't miss the exchange.

Answer this riddle: When is a liar no longer a liar? When is a thief no longer a thief? If you answered when he stops lying or when he stops stealing you're wrong. He may just be a liar or a thief taking a coffee break. A liar is no longer a liar when he has become a truth-teller. A thief is no longer a thief when he begins to earn rather than steal. That's a redeemed life.

He says, *Let no corrupting talk come out of your mouths, but only such as is good for building up, as fits the occasion, that it may give grace to those who hear (Ephesians 4:29).*

That can be very personal. The tongue is very sharp, very quick. Who amongst us can harness it? But why must we be concerned about what comes out of our mouths? Because we know from our former way of life — those of us who have been redeemed — we could say anything at any time, and it would be completely acceptable in the culture.

Culture isn't vague about what they think or feel. You can hear it in their speech. You can hear it in their profanity. You can hear it in their stories. That's all part of the old, former life. When you stop that type of talk, it testifies of the new clothing you've put on — *that it may give grace to those who hear.*

And do not grieve the Holy Spirit of God, by whom you were sealed for the day of redemption. Let all bitterness and wrath and anger and clamor and slander be put away from you, along with all malice. Be kind to one another, tenderhearted, forgiving one another, as God in Christ forgave you (Ephesians 4:30-32).

Very, very specific! Beloved, this is our calling. This is your calling. This is your role in sanctification: Put off the actions of the old self; renew the spirit of your mind with God's Word; put on the actions of the new self. To the end that we walk in a manner worthy of our calling, and that becomes a testimony of grace to those around us.

Our God has called us to a new life — a life of grace, faith, forgiveness and cleansing. We're not called to perfection — thank the Lord — because we'd fail miserably. It would have been over long ago.

No. He's called us by grace, to continue in grace. He is at work in us, to will and to work toward righteousness. He empowers us in our sanctification. In the synergism of it, we have responsibility. Will we do our part?

Let us not take lightly the precious gift of sanctification — this call. Let us walk in newness of life, to put on the garments of righteousness.

What say you?

www.ingramcontent.com/pod-product-compliance
Lightning Source LLC
Chambersburg PA
CBHW061103050726
47592CB00004B/1802